ESSENTIAL **DK** FINANCE

ONLINE
INVESTING

THERESA W. CAREY
AND
MARC ROBINSON

DORLING KI

London • New York • Sydney • Delh

D1305353

rg

A DORLING KINDERSLEY BOOK

Editor Stephanie Rubenstein
Writing Robert Lovka
Design and Layout Jill Dupont
Photography Anthony Nex
Project Editor Crystal A. Coble
Senior Art Editor Mandy Earey
Photo Research Mark Dennis, Sam Ruston
Indexing Rachel Rice
Editorial Director LaVonne Carlson
Design Director Tina Vaughan
Publisher Sean Moore

First American Edition, 2000
24681097531
Published in the United States by
Dorling Kindersley Publishing, Inc.
95 Madison Avenue,
New York, New York 10016

Packaged by Top Down Productions
Copyright © 2000
Dorling Kindersley Publishing, Inc.
Text copyright © 2000 Marc Robinson

**See our complete catalog at
www.dk.com**

A CIP catalogue record for this book is available from the Library of Congress

ISBN 0-7894-7176-0

Reproduced by Colourscan, Singapore
Printed by Wing King Tong, Hong Kong

CONTENTS

INTRODUCTION

Investing your money online can be very rewarding and may save you some money on commissions. Surely you've heard all the get-rich-quick advertisements for trading investments online. Unfortunately, many people have been lured into this arena by these ads without truly understanding what it takes and how to invest their money online. Online Investing gives you a basic understanding of what online investing is, how it works, and what you need to do it. It also dispels some myths about what you can actually do with your money online. After reading this book, you should have a good understanding of where to go to find an online broker, what to look for, how to make trades online, and who to turn to for help if you need it.

| 34 1! |
| 33 1 |

0.1125	-286.00	
13 11/16	-93.75	
27 15/16	225.00	
5 15/16	-187.00	
15 3/4	-124.80	
11 11/16	175.00	
0.0646	-1.75	
0.22	-105.00	

28 7/16	28
24 5/8	24
18 3/4	1

GETTING STARTED

Online investing puts you actively in charge
of your finances. This is as close as it gets
to do-it-yourself investing.

THE ONLINE REVOLUTION

Your home computer has leveled the investment playing field. Now anyone can access information that only a few years ago was available exclusively to stockbrokers and brokerage firms. You can act as your own stockbroker and your firm sits on top of your desk.

TAKING CONTROL

The Internet is now able to connect you to the securities markets. You only need an account with a broker, some money to invest, and the desire to research and track your own investments.

By investing online, you become your own money manager, assuming all the risks of investing. Depending on the brokerage firm you select, you may or may not have someone to advise you regarding your investing limits or to remind you of your needs and goals.

The ease of online investing can spur an investor toward increased trading, which studies now indicate, usually leads to lower annual returns on investments. Make sure you understand what you are doing.

GOOD REASONS TO INVEST ONLINE

There are a number of good reasons to invest online:

- You want to take active control of your investments;
- You can check stock quotes and market activity 24 hours a day;
- You can find out how overnight trading is affecting your stocks;
- You can monitor your portfolio and account at your convenience and as often as you wish;
- You have direct worldwide access to other investors, company information, and stock market research allowing you to plan your strategy at your convenience.

GOOD REASONS NOT TO INVEST ONLINE

There are also many misconceptions about online investing:

- You've heard that you can get rich quick;
- It's an entertaining, live-action computer game;
- It's an easy way to make some money.

WHO'S INVESTING ONLINE?

To many people, the image of an online investor is one of an aggressive day trader making, then losing, a fortune with many trades a day at the click of a mouse. In actuality, the profile is one of a middle-income investor with limited experience with investments.

◀ DESKTOP BROKER
Instead of a building made of bricks and mortar, your brokerage firm is housed in a computer that you control.

IT'S A FACT

By year-end 2000, it's expected that over $564 billion worth of investments will be managed in online investing accounts. By the end of 2001, that number is expected to reach nearly $1 trillion in 9.2 million active online accounts.

PREPARING THE COMPUTER

*T he personal computer has become an extraordinary investment tool.
Before you start investing online, make sure you're up to speed.*

HARD DRIVE

Your computer stores documents and applications on a disk located inside the computer. Since successful online investing is about research, analysis, and financial information, you will be creating many documents and storing many others. You will probably also be adding new financial software as you need it. All of this needs somewhere to call home, so there is no such thing as too much hard drive space. Ten to twenty gigabytes has become basic.

MONITOR

A large screen means less scrolling, and makes it easier to read spreadsheets and lists. A screen at least 17 inches (measured diagonally) will make investing life easier and allow for viewing multiple pages more efficiently. A big screen ultimately means less wrist work for you and is easier on your eyes when reading data and reports.

MEMORY

Your computer's Random Access Memory (RAM) is the memory available in your computer to run programs. The more RAM, the faster programs run. This is especially true when it comes to downloading web pages from any website's computer to your computer. If web pages take a long time to show up on your screen, the cause may be too little RAM.

You will want the ability to run tools such as a quote screen, a calculator, a news report, and maybe a stock ticker all at once. The minimum amount of RAM is 64 megabytes. Having 128 megabytes will make a big difference. Buy as much RAM as you can afford.

1 Your computer doesn't need super-enhancements for online investing.

2 Ask a prospective broker about their system requirements.

PROCESSOR

Basically the processor makes things run quickly. The faster your processor's speed, the faster the computer will complete its work, and the faster calculations and other tasks can be completed. The speed at which your computer's processor can execute instructions is measured in megahertz (MHz). You can speed through the world of online investing with a minimum 350 MHz processor.

BACK UP SYSTEM

Online investing means online financial records. Back up that all-important data onto a media outside your computer. Standard floppy disks aren't enough. A zip drive or a writable CD drive may be well worth the price.

pINTERNET CONNECTION

You need to have an account with an Internet service provider (the "phone company" of the Internet) who will hook you into the online world. The way you hook up is through a modem.

Dial-up modems. Most computers today come with built-in modems offering the speed of 56K (up to 56,000 bytes of information per second transferring into your computer from the Internet). To use these modems, you sign up for a dial-up account with the service provider, which means every time you want to connect to the Internet, you ask your modem to dial up the access number and make the connection.

Continuous connections. You can stay connected to the Internet 24 hours a day by signing up for access through cable (the same as TV cable) or DSL (which can go through your existing phone line without disrupting your regular phone service). Both of these connections can be up to 50 times faster than a 56K modem.

MYTHS VS. REALITIES

T*he Internet has spawned a giant world of information—and misinformation. What image of online investing do you have?*

GET IN, GET OUT, AND GET RICH QUICK!

Reality: Online investing is not the sure-fire road to riches people want to believe it is. In reality, the great majority of people who *day trade* (try to catch a rising stock then sell it in a day or two at a big profit) lose money. However, online investing can be a powerful financial tool for disciplined investors who make careful decisions based upon research and fact and own securities for more reasonable amounts of time. These are the same elements that make money for people through a traditional broker.

YOU GET THE HOT IPOS!

Reality: Initial Public Offerings (IPOs) are very difficult or impossible for small investors to acquire. Some online brokers have taken steps to offer them, but IPOs are still ruled by supply and demand (and the demand is high for a relatively small supply). Being online doesn't necessarily make it easier to acquire IPO shares.

BUY AND SELL 24 HOURS A DAY!

Reality: It depends on what you mean by "buy" and "sell." It's true that you can access your online account any hour of the day or night and put in an order. That doesn't necessarily mean you can execute a trade at any time. Many brokers now offer after-hours trading as a special service. However, the time is restricted to an hour or two before the markets open, and to a few hours after the markets close. It's a different type of trading and usually calls for a special access system. Full 24-hour trading may be a reality in the future. Basic trades you enter on your broker's site after market hours will normally be carried out when the market reopens.

◀ **NOT SO FAST**
You can burn a lot of money if you're looking to get rich quick online.

10

CLICK THE MOUSE AND THE SHARES ARE YOURS!

Reality: Clicking on BUY at your online broker's site does not mean that your order is filled at that particular moment. It means that it was ordered. During heavy trading periods in volatile markets your online order can be processed minutes or even hours later. Even though you saw your stock quoted at 20 a split second ago, your market order at 20 could be substantially more than that by the time your order is executed. Limit orders can help avoid being surprised by a higher price than you expected to pay (see pg. 42 for more on orders).

DON'TS AND DO'S

DON'T consider online investing the be-all, end-all. It can be a tool and component of any comprehensive investment plan.

DON'T put your life savings into an online account. Start small and build.

DON'T sell your long-held mutual funds to create cash for an online account. Mutual funds are convenient, long-term, agent-managed investments tailored for investors who haven't the time or expertise to actively pursue individual stocks and watch market activities. Managing an online portfolio of individual stocks is an active concern.

DON'T abandon your safe positions to pursue a new activity that may not suit you in the long run.

DO realize that problems are inevitable. As Murphy's Law says, "If anything can go wrong, it will," and Murphy loves technology! Your Internet connection can go down, the broker's server can crash, heavy trading can slow things down, etc. Be aware, and before selecting an online broker make sure it has alternative options for you.

DO diversify. Online investors tend to develop tunnel vision, concentrating their efforts in one sector of the market. Successful investing calls for balance, both in what you buy and also in how you buy it. If all your eggs are in one basket, what happens if you drop the basket? Stocks, bonds, mutual funds, and available savings all contribute to financial health. Online investing is one aspect of an overall financial plan. You should also have bank accounts, insurance, even a traditional brokerage account, and other vehicles to help you get where you're going.

DO your homework and **DO** your research. To succeed with any online investment it's important to be well informed about the company whose stock you're trading.

KNOW YOURSELF FIRST

B*e aware of the type of investor you are. It's as important to know why you're investing online as it is to know how to invest online.*

THE EMOTIONAL YOU

Your temperament can play a big part in your overall success in investing online. The online environment can be fast-paced and seductive.

Without an awareness of what you're doing, you could be swept up by emotion.

WHO ARE YOU?

These traits produce success in online investing. No one's perfect, but if you lack most of these traits you will need to be especially careful with your investing activity online.

Do you have:

● An interest in, and knowledge about, investing?

● Self-discipline?

● Emotional maturity?

● Good money-management skills?

● Organizational skills?

● An ability to face mistakes and learn from them.

THE BUSY YOU

Gauge how much time you have for the most important part of online investing—the homework. A quick click is only the tip of the online trading iceberg. A few minutes spent looking at your portfolio or at current stock quotes is generally not enough. Before the click comes the work of researching a stock, keeping abreast of the market, accessing news and analysis, and having the patience to wait. Then you need to be able to react at an opportune time to enter the market. All of this can be time-consuming work. Success in online investing requires a commitment of time and effort. Approach it as a new job. Will your online job be the first thing you do each morning, a lunch hour escape from your regular job, or an after-hours activity?

THE MATHEMATICAL YOU

Understanding how your investments are performing requires some basic arithmetic skills. Be sure you're comfortable interpreting tables and graphs before leaping online to trade.

ARE YOU CNBC OR ESPN?

Be attuned to your own emotional maturity. You can play all over the Internet. But playing at online investing is playing with your finances and your future. It can become a game—one you could lose. There's an exhilaration in playing the market and winning. Remember, though, your thrill of victory can turn into the agony of defeat quickly if you treat investing as a sport.

3 The fun factor and ease of trading make online investing seductive. Investors are often tempted to trade just for the fun of trading. Self-discipline will save you a lot of financial grief.

YOU THE INVESTOR

What kind of investor are you? In general, online investors fall into one of three categories:

Conservative cyberinvestors. The conservative online investor uses the Internet for its efficiency and access. Online accounts and investment news can be accessed quickly at any time. Yet, this investor wants some personal attention and guidance along the way from a broker. Conservatives can be new to investing or experienced traditionalists. They trade less frequently than the other two types.

Active onliners. This group is comfortable with being responsible for their own research, and interactions in the cyber environment. They trade on a consistent basis, holding some stocks for the long-term and holding others for a short-term changeover and profit. These cyberinvestors are online most days of the week, do their research, and monitor the market often.

Electronic traders. This group of active, aggressive speculators buy and sell most frequently to catch the upswings and downswings of the market, rather than hold positions and grow an investment. Day traders are the most active of this group. They transact trades continously throughout the day, taking risks, and piling up profits—and losses.

DEVELOP A PLAN

The reality is that online investing should be approached with caution. You should have a game plan.

A PLAN STARTS WITH AN IDEA

Go into online investing knowing why you're going there. Ask yourself why you are investing:
- Are you investing for the long- or short-term?
- Do you have a goal to achieve, such as a retirement objective, saving for a child's college tuition, or the great escape vacation?
- What's your plan and are you disciplined enough to follow through?

4 Be realistic. Investing, whether in the traditional mode or online, takes time, a plan, and discipline.

FINANCIAL CALCULATORS

It's easier to reach a goal when you have a specific picture in mind. For financial goals, a targeted sum of money takes the place of a mental picture. The Internet is full of free financial calculators that will calculate how much your investments and savings will have to grow in order to reach your targeted sum.

FinanCenter. This website at www.financenter.com allows you to fill-in blanks on a variety of ready-made forms that will do all the math and projections for you based on the information you enter.

Nasdaq. This market's website also has free financial calculators to help you plan ahead. Go to www.nasdaq.com, then link to "Investor Resources," click on "Financial Calculators" and pick one.

Others. Many other reliable calculators can be found at www.moneyadvisor.com.

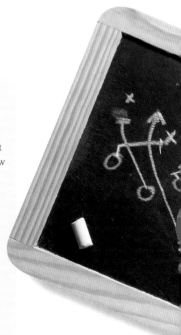

BE A GOAL-SETTER

Making investment goals keep you on track. This is especially important with online investing, which can become an entertainment or an escapist adventure. A goal-oriented financial plan consists of:

- Setting a goal;
- Developing a strategy for achieving that goal;
- Taking logical steps toward the goal;
- Honestly assessing your short-term results and making any necessary adjustments to your plan;
- Following through with the plan.

 5 Think, plan, do—and keep going!

THINGS TO KNOW

- Studies have shown the people who don't write down their goals have less chance of accomplishing them when compared to people who consistently write and update their goals.

- One calculator may come up with different solutions than another. It depends on how the calculator was programmed to interpret information. You may want to try the same calculation at a number of sites.

WHAT'S YOUR PLAN?

Any journey is easier with a roadmap. A financial plan is your map to financial success on the cyberhighway. Visualize your plan as three categories of investing:

- Cash savings for immediate needs and emergencies. This is money that does not go into the stock market;
- Short-term investing, such as for a house purchase, new auto, or accumulating money for a business;
- Long-term investing, such as for retirement or a college fund.

Write down your goals, calculate what it takes to accomplish them, then map out a strategy of investing in stocks, bonds, and mutual funds to achieve those goals.

FINDING AN ONLINE BROKER

You need an online brokerage firm to trade online.
This chapter will help you wade through the hype and
confusion to find a broker that suits you.

TRADITIONAL VS. ONLINE

You need an online broker to trade investments online. Your traditional broker may also have an online branch. Here is a comparison of online and traditional brokers.

IT'S ALL UP TO YOU

Online investing. You read the news, listen to tips, get interested in a stock (or any security), look for information, check out the company behind the stock, research stock market trends, try to predict price movements of the stock, and dream of getting rich. You decide on a stock to buy or sell. You decide how many shares you want to buy or sell. **Traditional investing.** Your broker and his professional research department do everything for you.

PLAYING BY THE RULES

Online brokers are subject to the same rules and regulations set for traditional brokers by the Securities and Exchange Commission (SEC). This is the regulatory arm of the federal government most responsible for protecting investors (see www.sec.gov). The SEC monitors trading activity and will act upon complaints against a brokerage firm. In addition, the National Association of Securities Dealers (NASD), a non-government group comprised of financial service firm members, sets industry standards and oversees securities dealers. See www.nasdr.org to check out a prospective broker.

THEN AND NOW
*Once upon a time you could only
invest by phone or in person. Today,
virtually everything you want to do
can be done with clicks of a mouse.*

THE BASIC COMPARISON

Traditional. Here are the basic elements of traditional trading (see pg. 42 for descriptions of the different types of orders):

- You tell the broker you want to buy (or sell) 100 shares of XYZ;
- The broker enters the trade "Buy 100 shares XYZ" into the firm's order system;
- The order is sent through the system to a trading exchange (the store selling the product: stocks and other securities);
- The trading system (human or electronic) fills an order for 100 shares of XYZ;
- There may be hundreds of orders for XYZ at the exchange. Each time someone buys or sells some XYZ, the price of it moves up or down. Your order for XYZ waits in line for its turn to be filled (executed) at the current price (if it's a market order) or until it hits a price you indicate (if it's a limit or stop order);
- 100 shares of XYZ are sent back to your broker and appear as an entry in your account.

- If you're buying, you pay for 100 shares, plus a commission for the broker's services, and for using the system, along with any taxes on the transaction;
- If you're selling, you receive money for selling XYZ, plus also pay a commission and taxes.

Online. Guess what? The same thing happens! Except you enter the order information into the system and click your mouse, sending the order on its way.

IT'S A FACT

The first electronic investing offered to investors was through limited touch-tone telephone trading in the 1980s.

TYPES OF BROKERS

There are approximately 200 online brokerages to choose from with features and benefits that change constantly. Here are some issues to consider.

THE MAIN TYPES

Online brokers fall into the same categories as traditional brokers.

Full-service. These brokers are the latest entrants into the online world. They offer traditional management, hand holding, and advice. You can browse through their extensive research reports online.

Discount. These brokers offer little or no personal contact and advice. Some research and information is available, but you may pay extra for comprehensive research.

Deep discount. These brokers are basically no frills. Quotes and news are part of your package, but you're on your own at rock-bottom commissions.

Combinations. Keep in mind that the category boundaries aren't neatly drawn and will probably continue to blur as time goes on and competition and innovation evolve. For example, a full-service firm may offer some discount programs and a discount firm may offer virtually full-service treatment for a fee.

6 Many brokers offer real-time online chat with their customer service representatives.

INVESTORS BEWARE

Watch out for the hype. Brokers are flocking to the Internet and advertising their services with messages touting everything from the ease and fun of trading stocks to hinting at how easy it is to get rich with them. It's up to you to wade through that and find a broker who fits your investment style—just like you should do with traditional brokerage firms. For example:

- Do you want personal attention?
- How about research reports on companies you're thinking of buying? Will you have to buy the reports?
- Do you want access to mutual funds? Can they buy the one you want?
- How financially secure is the broker? Review the brokerage firm's financial statement. Read it like you would any corporate financial statement.
- Is there any disciplinary action against this broker? You can check that out online at www.nasdr.org.

OPENING QUESTIONS

Before signing on the electronic dotted line, consider your particular style of investing, experience, and temperament:

- How much buying and selling will you do?
- Do you want someone to give you direction and advice?
- Are you going to make basic or complex trades?

DO YOU WANT TO TRADE BONDS?

Many online brokers don't offer bond trading online. Your online account may still be able to accommodate bond trading, but require you to make the trade with a person via the telephone. Bond trading online is growing as the technology for managing the inventory improves.

▲ BALANCING ACT
Selecting an online broker may be more of a balancing act than choosing a traditional broker. You have to consider how good you are at making investment decisions.

CUSTOMER SERVICE

Online brokers have widely differing ideas about what constitutes customer service:

- Is there a person you can telephone at no extra fee to help when something goes wrong?
- What does the technical support entail?
- Is there a branch office you can go to?

Telephone queries to an online broker can be frustrating. Complaints about a site crash, technical problem, or trading error can result in the same delays experienced with any business. However, these delays may cost you money in lost trades. Some can take a day or more to answer your e-mail queries.

19

COMPETITIVE FACTORS

*W*hat do online brokers offer? Every brokerage firm is slightly different. Finding the right mix of services, products, price, and reliability that are best for you is a challenge. Deciding what's important to you first, can make it easier. Consider this checklist of factors and potential problems.

WEBSITE DESIGN

Your broker's website should be easy to understand, easy to use, and load pages quickly.

Clarity. Too many glitzy graphics on a website can slow things down and make navigation difficult.

Speed. The best websites come up within 2-4 seconds. Many investors will give up if it takes 8 seconds. There are no SEC regulations requiring a trade to be executed in a certain amount of time. Speed depends on your broker's system and ability to service you.

SECURITY

Know what protections the brokerage firm has in place to ensure private, accurate, and safe trading. Your finances are in cyberspace. Know how they're protected.

SPECIALTY TRADING

What does the broker offer?
- Are after-hours trading, day trading, IPOs, bonds, options, and mutual funds trading available?
- Are there extra charges for these types of trades?

COSTS

Low commissions are not the best criteria for selecting a broker. There can be additional charges for certain orders and services, maintenance and transfer fees, and many little surprises. In general, you get what you pay for.

INITIAL DEPOSITS/ ACCOUNT BALANCES

Ask about basic account requirements:
- How much will it take to open an account? Deposits can range from a few hundred to several thousands of dollars;
- Can you receive bonus services like free real-time quotes, premium research, or a number of commission-free trades by maintaining a large balance in your account?
- How quickly will your deposit show in your account?

WHAT'S MOST IMPORTANT?

A reliable trading system, speedy access, and low commissions are the things investors want most from an online firm.

EXECUTIONS AND CONFIRMATIONS

Ask a prospective broker:

- How its system will react to heavy volume.
- Is there a recent history of downtime?
- Will the broker compensate you (free trades or other services) if you can't access his system to make your trades?

QUOTES

How will you be able to read stock price quotes? Do they offer:

Standard quotes. This reflects a delay of 15-20 minutes from the time they were actually in effect;

Real-time quotes. This quotes you the most immediate price of a stock;

Streaming. This runs a ticker tape across your screen in either real-time or standard delay.

How important is it for you to have real-time or streaming quotes? These services can cost extra, or be limited to a certain number for which you pay a fee. The good news is that free real-time quotes are available on the Internet at many financial websites. You can find them at www.freerealtime.com and www.quote.com.

OTHER FINANCIAL SERVICES

Some brokers offer Internet banking services for your online account. Debit cards, ATMs, check-writing, online bill-paying, mortgage, and insurance services all build a bridge between banking and your investment portfolio.

RESEARCH AND EDUCATION

If you're going to be investing online, whether or not you have prior investing experience, ask if:

- The broker offers its own or a third-party provider's research and stock news to you at no charge;
- There's any type of tutorial or educational learning center about investing on its site or is there a link to one.

MISCONCEPTIONS AND MISUNDERSTANDINGS

You see the ads, look at the site, and think you've found a home. But can you be sure?

1. LOW ADVERTISED COST MAY NOT BE AS LOW FOR YOU

Look beyond the advertised price. It may only apply to trades larger than you want to make—possibly hundreds of shares. Find out what the commission will be for your trade and if rates apply only to trading stocks in a specified price range.

2. "NO DEPOSIT" STILL MEANS A DEPOSIT

Some brokers advertise "no minimum deposit" to open an account. Literally, that's true. You can fill out the application and open an account. You just can't trade with it! For trading you will need funds in the account or a credit line. A few brokers now offer immediate trading if you can qualify following a credit check.

3. THERE'S TRADING AND SPECIALTY TRADING

Not all brokers offer access to all the different kinds of securities. If you're a regular investor in IPOs, bonds, options, mutual funds, or want to engage in some more sophisticated trading such as short sales, ask a prospective broker if the firm can support your kind of trading. Availability differs significantly.

4. DIRECT MAY NOT BE INSTANT

Click and trade? Maybe. Most brokerage firms have a security program that flags trades for review before sending them to the exchange. This can cause a short delay in your order being executed, but may assure that trades made in your account fit your investment profile.

> **7** Make a list of which factors you must have and which are borderline. This will help define the broker you eventually select.

> **8** Beware of brokers claiming guaranteed returns on your stock investments. This claim is illegal.

5. DIFFERENT FIRMS OFFER DIFFERENT TRADING PERKS

If you expect to buy and sell frequently, look for a broker who will reward you with lower commissions, free trades, or other perks. Each broker defines "frequently" differently. Make sure the broker's definition coincides with yours.

6. RESEARCH QUALITY VARIES

Some brokers give you valuable research charts, news, elaborate portfolio trackers, and other tools free of charge. Others charge extra for these services.

7. CUSTOMER SERVICE IS ALL THE SAME

People take for granted that online brokers offer 24 hour, 7-day a week support. Don't awaken to a surprise when you need help most. Find out about support policies up front. Make sure you can speak face-to-face with someone in an office.

8. ALL YOUR EGGS DON'T HAVE TO BE IN ONE BASKET

A backup broker—as well as a backup system for accessing the Internet—can be invaluable if your primary source is hit with technical problems or heavy trading delays.

9. STANDARDS AND SECURITY VARY

Bottom-fishing for the lowest commission rates can be hazardous. Be sure the brokerage firm is a member of the National Association of Securities Dealers (NASD) and Securities Investment Protection Corporation (SIPC). Be sure your broker's trading system is secure. Look for the padlock icon on your browser's status bar (at the bottom).

◀ THE PADLOCK
Look for this symbol in the lower left corner of the browser window. If the lock is closed, the website is secure.

WHAT PRODUCTS AND SERVICES ARE OFFERED?

Each online broker can differ in the types of trading, services, and support available to you. It's important to find the right mix of services balanced against cost and your needs. Here's what you can expect to find.

BASIC TRADING

All online brokers allow you to buy and sell stocks listed on the major exchanges. U.S. Treasury securities and IRA accounts are also generally available everywhere. Brokers will offer option trading as a special service. Mutual funds trading is widely available, but the number and types of funds available to trade differ from broker to broker. If you're interested in trading penny stocks, ask specifically if you can buy them through a prospective broker.

ALTERNATE WAYS TO PLACE TRADES

Besides your computer and the broker's online trading screens, there may be alternate systems you can use to make a trade in case of an online breakdown or access delays. Not all online firms accommodate touch-tone telephone trading, and broker-assisted trades could mean additional commissions or fees. Ask about the alternate systems and charges before signing up.

SPECIALTY TRADING

Online brokers services differ widely. They may offer specialties such as short-selling, access to IPOs, Nasdaq Level II screen access, and after-hours trading. How important is it to you to engage in these types of trades? Your answer will narrow your list of suitable brokers.

More and more brokers are offering access to after-hours trading, but your access times could be significantly restricted. One firm's definition of after-hours might mean trading only between 4:15 and 6:30 pm, while another's definition may mean trading during a ninety-minute pre-market-opening period and a four-hour trading period after the final bell. A higher commission rate usually applies.

9 "Free services/Low costs" ads may only apply to accounts with minimum balance requirements of $10,000 or more.

PORTFOLIO UPDATES

Brokers handle portfolio updates in different ways. Find out how frequently during the day stock prices and portfolio values are updated. Some brokers will even supply e-mail updates of breaking news about your stocks. These services may be quite valuable.

WHAT ABOUT WIRELESS?

The latest advance to online trading is the use of smart phones or pagers to make trades. Highly aggressive traders like the anytime/anywhere access, but the cost for a suitable device can be hundreds of dollars. In addition, with the monthly usage fees this can be trading overkill for the small investor.

INVESTMENT TOOLS

Investment tools are the real-time quotes, portfolio update services, market research, stock news, technical charts, and portfolio management bells and whistles that brokers offer as part of an account. The lowest-commissioned accounts will have fewer, and less elaborate versions of these services for you.

BANKING SERVICES

Many online brokers now offer banking services such as check writing, debit cards, mortgage services, and loans as part of your investment account. The most important banking service they can offer is a system that sweeps your cash balances into an interest-earning account. Cash in your online account should be working for you!

◀ WELCOME HOME
You can get a fairly good sense of the range of products and services offered simply by looking at an online broker's home page. In fact, if a home page doesn't provide a broad overview and a lot of opportunities for you to move around the site, it may be a forewarning of things to come inside.

COSTS AND FEES

T he broker with the lowest commission rates could turn out to be the most expensive broker for your individual needs. With online commissions, costs, and fees, there's more than meets the eye.

IT's A FACT

In 2000, commissions online were about 44% less than the average commissions charged by offline discount brokers, and about 80% less than full-service.

ACCOUNT FEES

You may encounter additional fees for administrative services. Online brokers can charge you for stock certificate delivery, wire transfer of funds, IRA setup and maintenance, extra copies of statements, documentation fees, e-mail confirmations, and dozens of other services. Fees and charges should be listed on a broker's site and sent with the application form sent to you by mail. Make sure you understand these costs before committing to a broker. Bookkeeping fees, accounting fees, and special service fees can turn a low-cost dream into an expensive proposition.

COMMISSIONS

The most advertised feature of online trading may be the low commission rates. Look closely at the rate, however. That $7.95 figure could apply only to a simple market order to trade a listed stock on a major exchange. In addition, the low rate is typically for either the buy or the sell, not both.

A broker's lowest advertised commission rate may be tied to the number of trades you make over a specified period of time. For example, the first 30 trades during a 3-month period could be $14.95, but any after that would be at a different rate. Ask what restrictions apply to the lowest rate.

---

10 If a broker's fee schedule isn't posted online, ask for one to be e-mailed to you before opening the account.

---

11 Placing limit , stop , after-hours , or option orders can cost you a higher commission rate at nearly all the brokerage firms.

SPECIAL SERVICE FEES

In general, the lower the commission, the higher and more numerous the broker's fees. There are many different possibilities. Many brokers charge you to place a trade over the telephone, make a broker-assisted trade, redeem bonds, access the firm's own research, receive real-time quotes, and place orders other than market orders.

RESEARCH AND INVESTMENT TOOLS

Nearly all accounts come with some type of market news and portfolio management tools. Technical charts, stock analyses, sector analyses, and so-called "premium research," however, often cost extra. Whatever is a cost at one firm may be free at another. Consider the range of materials and tools offered before signing up.

SIGN-UP DISCOUNTS

Competition for your online business is always an issue, so brokers periodically will offer discounts or other perks such as limited commission-free trades (e.g., first five trades free), waivers of certain accounting fees, or other inducements that will reduce your overall costs *temporarily*. Read the fine print to determine the extent of the actual discounts and the length of time they will apply.

12 Low commission rates may be worthless if you can't make your trades quickly and efficiently. Reliability and service outweigh low rates.

13 Even the lowest commission costs add up. Aggressive buying and selling often offsets any savings from the frequent-trader rate.

THINGS TO KNOW

- Fees and commissions usually have a lot to do with how good a customer you are to the firm. Online brokers often reduce commissions for customers who trade often. Ask for a rate break tailored to your trading frequency.

- If you have a large account (over $100,000) you might want to look for a broker who will give you access to premium research for free.

- The size of an order can also affect commission rates. A firm may charge a higher-than-advertised rate for large orders. This can apply to orders of 1,000, 5,000, or more shares traded at one time. As usual, brokers define *large* in their own terms. Get to know the concept of *block trading* if you're planning to buy or sell large amounts of stock.

CUSTOMER SERVICE

*I*t's a cyberworld, but when problems arise you may want a person to talk to. In choosing a broker, how important it is for you to have a personal connection?

MORE INVESTING, MORE SERVICE

The more you invest, the more contact you will probably have with a broker's customer service department. If problems can't be resolved through e-mail, you will be forced to try phone calls. (You may prefer that route.) Choose a broker who specifies 24-hour, 7-day a week customer service support. Try it out to confirm that matters can be handled at all times, and that you're not put on a list for callbacks during regular hours.

QUALITY VARIES

Online investing is still in its infancy and problems with trading this way are still surfacing. Broker responses to problems vary greatly. Some don't want to hear from you at all; ("It's an online service; please contact us through e-mail"). All brokers offer technical support via e-mail, but few will guarantee a response during the same day.

A broker's customer service reps must be licensed. The training and certification process takes months. The explosive growth of online investing has outpaced the staffing of customer service areas. Committed hiring efforts promise to alleviate some problems. Check the broker's website and sales literature for a customer service phone number. If it's not toll-free, beware.

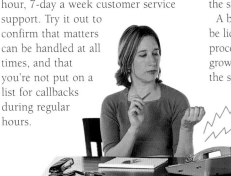

◀ WHO CARES?

Being online can take on a whole new meaning when you listen to lengthy ringing or on-hold music. Many businesses—in every aspect of the financial cyberworld—may understaff their customer service departments or hire underqualified, undertrained, and/or apathetic applicants.

BIGGER, OLDER, BETTER?

Old-line, full-service brokerage firms are marching online. These firms have experience with customer problems and should offer you consistent service.

Low fees, rock-bottom commissions, and free trades might translate into reduced customer service. An online brokerage is a business and needs to make money. Low costs set the stage for low profit margins. The answer is usually a cut in overhead, which often results in few customer service reps to help you iron out problems over the phone, by e-mail, or in person.

Firms with long standing track records may have an edge in the online market. However, with new technologies and innovations, the field is changing rapidly and constantly. Newer firms may be able to compete with the old ones quite well.

MARKET TIMING

Service that's 24/7 allows you to avoid the crowded market time calling that results in frustrating delays. The opening and closing hours of the market are the busiest trading times. People aren't as likely to call at midnight as they are at noon. Take advantage of this.

TEST THE SYSTEM

Get an idea of a broker's customer service capabilities by calling its customer service 800 number and talking to a representative. Consider:
- How long did it take to get through?
- Are you routed through a system of "Press 1 for..."? If your broker uses electronic answering, you can be stuck wading through a menu of services meant for general, prospective-customer routing. Have your account number ready to punch into the system when first prompted. This may bypass the generic instructions and menus.
- Can you get clear answers to questions about the firm, its customer service policies, etc.?
- Were they friendly and helpful or short with you?
- Can the rep handle your questions or are there further routings?

Also try the e-mail system. Ask a simple question about their service or products or request an application kit. How long did it take them to get back to you?

---

14 Poor customer service is the number one complaint investors lodge against their online brokers.

15 If you place emphasis on personal service, choose a broker with an office you can visit.

SAFETY AND SECURITY

O nline investing is getting safer all the time. Layers of protection, coding, and insurance exist to guarantee and protect your account.

BROKER SECURITY

Safe information transfer systems over the web are continually improving. Any decent broker will likely use a process of *encryption* that changes your data into a form that can be read only by the intended receiver with the proper encryption key.

What is encryption? All of the communications between you and your broker are scrambled into a jumble of letters and symbols that would look like gibberish if intercepted by a hacker. The broker's electronic system acts as a decoder to process your instructions.

While no broker can provide a 100% guarantee against a hacker's invasion, some brokers may use multiple levels of encryption and multiple security systems to complicate any potential intrusion and thereby increase their customers' protection.

You won't lose funds. A hacker raid on your account most likely won't result in a withdrawal of funds. You're the only person who can order money or securities withdrawn from the account, which must be done by written, signed instructions. For verification, your signature is required to be on file with the broker when you open an account.

INSURANCE

Securities. Any broker you work with should be a member of the Securities Investor Protection Corporation (SIPC). It's a private organization that protects you against a firm going bankrupt or not being able to protect your assets. SIPC insures each account up to $500,000 for securities and $100,000 for cash. Ask whether your broker carries additional insurance to cover account assets over $500,000 and against disasters such as fire. Look for reference to SIPC on the brokers' ads and application forms.

Banking. If your broker provides banking services, it should offer the same federal insurance protection you would get at a traditional bank.

SYSTEM FAILURES

Site crashes and electronic glitches do happen, but they're not normally something you have financial recourse against. Your best protection against a site being down is to have a second broker to contact for trades. Ask any prospective broker how they handle downtime:

- Are phone-in orders taken at no extra fee?
- Can you fax an order to them?
- Does the broker have a nearby office you can visit in person?

PASSWORDS AND PINS

Your online broker will require you to enter your individual password and account number before you can access your account—no codes, no access! This cybersystem is actually superior to the traditional system in which a phone call and persuasive voice can get past a human on the other end. Guard your passwords and PINS.

◀ LOCK OUT
To protect access to your account, online brokers employ a firewall—a special software designed to foil intruders.

16 Be sure to use the latest browser from companies such as Netscape, AOL, or Microsoft to ensure that you're using the latest in online security technology. They're available for free at their home websites.

CONSTANT MONITORING

Most likely, your trading account will be monitored continuously by a security system that flags any unusual trading activity, guarding against unauthorized use of your account. The system will alert a broker, who should then call you to ask if you ordered the unusual-looking trade.

17 A brokerage firm will guarantee you a secure user name and account password that must be used to access your account.

WAYS TO COMPARE

With so many online brokers offering so many different combinations of products and services, it can be overwhelming finding a broker who fits your needs. Fortunately, there are a wide variety of online services created specifically to help people like you.

COMPARISONS AND RANKINGS

There are some independent research firms offering extensive comparisons and rankings of online brokers.

Gomez Advisors. This website lets you select two broker names at a time from a drop-down menu, then click on a "Compare" button. A sheet appears listing what each firm offers under 14 categories of criteria ranging from deposits required to products and services offered. Gomez also provides scorecards on brokers with comments about their services and ranks brokers according to a wide variety of criteria. Access their free services at www.gomez.com.

Weiss Ratings Inc. This website ranks online brokers on safety and financial stability. You can access their reports for free at www.weissratings.com.

Barron's. This firms financial newspaper, annually ranks online brokers on suitability for high net worth individuals. See *The Electronic Investor* at www.barrons.com.

STOPWATCH TIMING

While all brokers claim to make fast, accurate trading available to you, Keynote actually measures the timeliness, speed and accuracy of online brokers. You can access their Broker Trading Index and get the lowdown on speed and performance at www.keynote.com.

MATCHING SERVICE

One way to find a broker who matches your needs is to use the free "Online Broker Decision Maker" at www.xolia.com. You will be asked to complete a questionnaire that rates various services and product availability. The system then lists brokers who fit your own criteria.

TRACK RECORDS

Check on any history of problems that investors have had with a firm at the NASD website—www.nasdr.com. Records of regulatory and disciplinary actions against firms are usually listed there.

IT'S A FACT

Ninety percent of the online investing market is shared by ten firms.

THE HANDS-ON APPROACH

Many brokerage sites have trading demos that allow you to experience how trading works on their site. You can operate screens, place mock trades, and see how the process works. You can use the demos as a final check before committing any money to a particular broker.

GOING FOR GOSSIP ▼
Online chat rooms and bulletin boards have become popular ways for people to spread and receive opinions without having their comments filtered. Beware, though, of deliberate attempts to inflate or deflate public opinion.

18 The best broker for you is ultimately a matter of your own style and taste. In the final comparisons, trust your feelings.

TAP PUBLIC OPINION

Both online and offline financial magazines regularly rate the performance of online brokers. Many investors are willing to talk—and complain—about their online brokers.

To get the word of mouth on a firm, log on to one of many investor chat rooms on the Internet. Yahoo! has an extensive investor/financial/business area that includes many chat rooms and bulletin boards. The Lycos network's Quote.com (www.quote.com) is one forum, or you can try Motley Fool (www.fool.com) or Raging Bull (www.ragingbull.com).

OPENING AN ACCOUNT

After comparison shopping, you're ready to commit to an online broker. Applying is simple, but pay attention to the fine print.

TYPES OF ACCOUNTS

Cash account. You pay as you go with funds you deposit in your account.

Margin account. With this account, you can borrow money from your broker to buy securities. You're basically buying stocks on credit with the stock purchased serving as collateral. Interest is charged on your loan. Be wary about opening a margin account. If the value of your holdings drops below a certain level, your account can be liquidated to satisfy the shortfall.

Option account. This is a type of margin account that allows specialized trading in options.

IRA/Retirement/401k accounts. These are special accounts with specific restrictions.

IN A HURRY?

If you're in a hurry and must have immediate trading, you may be best off stopping for a moment to consider your motives. What's the rush? The smartest way to invest online is based on a plan or for convenience. Your immediate emotionally-based factors can be dangerous and costly.

TYPES OF OWNERSHIP

You may open one or more of the following types of brokerage accounts. Each type specifies how and who owns the assets in the account, and will dictate some restrictions placed on the terms of that ownership.

Individual. Only you can access the account.

Joint. More than one person can access the account.

Custodial. You manage an account for a minor.

Trust. The account is managed as a trust for one or more beneficiaries.

19 Persons under age 18 (or 21 in some states) may not manage their own investment accounts.

20 By law, all brokers—online and traditional—must require you to fill out a formal application to open an account.

THE APPLICATION AND DEPOSIT

In order to trade with a broker, you're typically required to have a signed application, agreement, and deposit on file.

Initial deposits. An initial deposit to open your online account can range from $500 to $10,000 depending on the firm. The average requirement is $1,000-$2,000.

Your application. Applications are subject to a credit and background check and determination of your net worth before final approval is granted. With great credit and a solid net worth, you can receive fast approval. Many applications require further investigation before being approved.

Special offers. You may be able to trade online immediately. Securities regulations require trades to be settled (funds received) within three days of the trade taking place. Therefore, you can open an account and make trades the same day, but you must send money to cover your transactions and assure that the money will arrive at the brokerage firm within three business days. Some brokers let you set up immediate electronic links to your checking account.

21 Some online brokers automatically open your account as a margin account unless you specify otherwise. Read the application carefully and know what you're signing.

▼ THE ACCOUNT SCREEN
Here is an example of what you might see online as an account application. As the instructions say, you must choose one type of account. You may be able to open as many types of accounts as you want (depending upon your approval status), but you will need to repeat the application process separately for each account.

CHOOSE ACCOUNT TYPE (select one of each)	
SELECT ONE	**Asset Class**
⊙	**Futures Only**
⊙	**Long Options Only**
⊙	**Futures and Options**
⊙	**US Stocks Only -- Cash Account**
⊙	**US Stocks Only -- Margin Account**
⊙	**US Stocks, Stock Options and Stock Index Options -- Margin Account**

UNDERSTANDING YOUR AGREEMENT

*T*he agreement of terms between you and your broker is extensive. The agreement should be posted on the broker's website. Pay attention to it because it can have profound implications for your account. Here are some of the key points in most agreements.

INVESTOR PROFILE

Broker applications used to contain a section asking you about your financial condition and investing experience. This section reflected a rule enacted by the NYSE and NASD to ensure that a broker's investment recommendations were suitable for a client's objectives and risk tolerance.

Today, many online trading firms have dropped this section from their applications, seeing no need for it if they're not recommending specific investments—only executing trades.

If your application does contain this section, complete it truthfully. In the long run, this profile could aid you in case of legal disputes against the broker.

---

22 One advantage of online over traditional brokerage relationships is that you can always read standard account agreements online.

CREDIT CARD BUYS

A few online brokerage firms may allow you to use a credit card to buy stocks. Keep in mind that you will be borrowing money to buy securities that could lose value even before you've paid for them—and the interest rate may be high.

DISPUTE PROVISIONS

In an attempt to limit lawsuits and legal fees, many online brokers require new customers to sign an agreement that sends disputes to an arbitration board rather than to an open court of law. Arbitration saves legal fees, but statistics indicate that disputing customers believe they have won less often than they deserved to win.

MARGIN MAXIMS

If you open a margin account understand that:

- You're paying interest, usually compounded daily, on the money you borrow;
- You can lose more money than you originally invested;
- On short notice, you can be required to deposit additional cash or securities to cover losses in your account;
- You can be forced to sell securities;
- Your broker has the right to sell your securities without consulting you.

---

23 Make copies of all agreements, e-mails, and applications from your broker. A paper file is essential in case of disputes.

MARGIN RULES

Minimum. Before trading on margin, the NYSE and NASD, require you to deposit a minimum of $2,000 with your brokerage firm or 100% of the purchase price of the stock you're buying, whichever is less. This is known as the *minimum margin*. Some firms may require more.

Maximum. Federal regulations allow you to borrow up to 50% of the purchase price of securities that are permitted to be purchased on margin. This is known as the *initial margin*. Some firms may require more. Not all securities may be purchased on margin.

Maintenance margin. After you buy stock on margin, the NYSE and NASD require you to have cash equal to at least 25% of the total market value of the securities in your margin account at all times. This is called the *maintenance requirement*. Many firms have higher requirements.

CLOSING AN ACCOUNT MAY BE DIFFICULT

Opening an account is easy, but closing one can be another matter. Fund transfers to a new broker often run into bureaucratic delays. You may need to write and sign a hard copy letter, face a few weeks of paper shuffling and transfer procedures, pay a transfer fee, and still have loose ends to deal with if a dividend or credit arrives in the middle of or after the process. The moral is, choose your broker carefully at the outset—but don't be afraid to move on if your broker's service isn't what you need.

STARTING TO INVEST

Online investing is a world offering sophisticated tools for research, analysis, and trading designed to turn you into your own stockbroker.

INVESTOR EDUCATION

*P*ossibly the biggest risk you face in online investing is jumping in without understanding personal finance and the way investing works.

FROM THE BROKER

Your online brokerage should have an education area on its website. You should be able to find helpful information on basic investing, an overview of personal finance, and what elements make for a sound investment. Be aware, though, that brokerage firms are famous for slanting educational material to suit their own needs. It's possible that the information will be biased.

FROM THE EXCHANGES

The major stock exchanges provide extensive educational information on the workings of a stock market and advice on finding sound investments. Here are some key websites:
- The New York Stock Exchange (www.nyse.com);
- Nasdaq (www.nasdaq.com);
- The American Stock Exchange (www.amex.com).

 24 Many brokers have tours so you can preview their site before you sign on.

FROM INDEPENDENT SITES

Hundreds of websites can open your eyes to the inner workings of investing. Successful investors never stop learning. Keep learning, even if you think you know it all. Here are some good websites to know:

- The American Association of Individual Investors (www.aaii.com) is full of valuable advice on the business of investing;
- The League of American Investors (www.investorsleague.com) also offers unbiased educational information and an interactive stock market game that serves as an investing tool for small investors;
- Financial terminology and the concepts behind the terms are explained in plain English (www.investopedia.com);
- What criteria do you use to pick sound stocks? Teach Me Finance (www.teachmefinance.com) explains basic financial concepts, including stock valuations, bond valuations, money dynamics, interest rates, future values of investments, and how to analyze a company's true value.

THE FUN EXCHANGE

You can have fun learning about the dynamics of a stock market at The Hollywood Stock Exchange (www.hsx.com). "buy" into Steven Speilberg's latest movie or "sell" off your shares of Liv Tyler for Cameron Diaz instead!

FROM PROFESSIONAL ADVISORS

If navigating the world of finance seems a daunting task, financial advisors can make the journey less confusing. A starting point for choosing a financial advisor or financial planner is the Certified Financial Planner Board of Standards (www.cfp-board.org), a nonprofit, professional regulatory organization that certifies and licenses financial planners. They can give you a list of certified advisors in your area and advice on what to look for in an advisor.

MAKING A TRADE:
THE ORDER SCREENS

Each brokerage will have its own style of ordering screens which you will operate, but all will be a version of the same basic features allowing you to place an order. Here is an example of how you make a trade online.

1. START AT HOME

Go to your broker's site online—all brokers have some type of home page. This can be a simple welcome page or an elaborate one containing access to streaming quotes, links to research, news, and so on. To begin the order process, click on the account LOGIN.

2. LOG IN

Enter your identification (usually your user ID and password) and click.

3. PREPARE AN ORDER

You will find access to ORDER ENTRY. Depending on the broker, this page can offer you much more than just ordering. There can be links to specific research, charts, market information, and price quotes about the company you're about to buy or sell for up-to-date information.

4. ENTER AN ORDER

After signing in, click on the ENTER ORDER, PREVIEW ORDER. or SUBMIT button (whichever one your broker has on its site) to indicate you're entering an order. Clicking on this button sends you to the next screen.

5. DO A DOUBLE-CHECK

A PREVIEW ORDER screen comes up and lists the trade as you've entered it. This is where you verify that the information is correct. Pay careful attention to the PREVIEW ORDER screen. It's your final opportunity to catch mistakes. An errant keyboard stroke in entering your order information can turn your 100-share buy into 1,000 shares. You will, however, usually be shown the total cost of the trade.

6A. PLACE THE ORDER

Clicking on the PLACE ORDER/ SUBMIT/CONFIRM button sends the trade, as previewed, on its way.

 OR

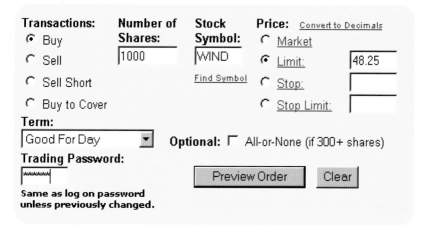

Transactions:	Number of Shares:	Stock Symbol:	Price: Convert to Decimals	
⦿ Buy			○ Market	
○ Sell	`1000`	`WIND`	⦿ Limit:	`48.25`
○ Sell Short		Find Symbol	○ Stop:	
○ Buy to Cover			○ Stop Limit:	

Term:
`Good For Day` ▼   **Optional:** ☐ All-or-None (if 300+ shares)

Trading Password:
`******`

[Preview Order]   [Clear]

Same as log on password
unless previously changed.

▲ **TRADING SCREEN**
This is a sample of a trading screen, which can vary greatly from broker to broker.

6B. CANCEL THE ORDER

A CANCEL ORDER button will take you back to the ordering screen to reenter or change information. The ordering process can take less than a minute. You will find CANCEL ORDER buttons on the Confirmation/Verification screens and on your personal portfolio screens. A trade can be cancelled, but only if it hasn't already been executed in the market.

7A. RECEIVE A CONFIRMATION

Finally, a page indicating that your trade has been accepted and sent comes up. It may be a simple label saying ORDER CONFIRMED, a verification of the order telling you the exact time it was accepted, or just a screen asking if you wish to place another trade.

7B. CONFIRM THE TRADE YOURSELF

Most online brokers send you an e-mail confirmation when your trade is executed, but some confirm only that the order was made. Viewing your portfolio page shows whether your action was completed. But if your account is not serviced with real-time updating, you will have to rely on the Transaction History or Order Status screens to show you where you stand.

CONTROLLING TRADES

You can control your trading through pricing and timing.

CONTROLLING PRICING

Here's an overview of how you can control the price of your trade.

Market order. This is a request for your order to be executed at the price available at the time your trade is ready to be filled. Placing a market order online, therefore, doesn't give you control over the price you receive. In a fast-moving market, for example, your order could be filled at a price that's considerably different than you expected.

A broker's low advertised commission usually is available only for market orders.

Limit orders. This order tells your broker only to make your trade at—or better than—the price you designate. Limit orders are commonly used in online trading. There are drawbacks however. If your price is not met, the order will not be filled. Even online, you may not get your trade if other orders at that price are ahead of yours.

Commissions on limit orders are typically higher than those for market orders.

Stop orders. This tells your broker to make the trade only if the price hits a level you specify (the stop price) or better—but only after the stop price has been reached or exceeded. In effect, a stop order is a flexible limit order that

> **25** Remember each time you click ORDER, you're charged fees. Mistakes can be very expensive.

may give you a tight range of prices in which your order can be placed. There are a variety of stop orders, but most online brokers offer only the most basic. Ask your broker what kinds of stop orders s/he offers.

Like limit orders, stop orders typically have higher commissions than the basic market orders.

Options. Brokers will offer options trading as a special service and provide you with special screens.

Commissions vary based on the number and price of the options.

Short sales. A short sale is when you sell stock you don't own and then buy it later. You're betting that the price will drop and allow you to buy the stock later at a lower price, repay your broker, and keep the rest of what you were paid as your profit. Some brokers don't allow you to sell short. Others may offer short sale orders, but will delay executing the order until you confirm it by telephone.

CONTROLLING TIMING

Order screens will ask how long you want your order to stay in effect.

Day orders. A day order remains active only for the day it was entered on the screen.

Good Til Cancelled (GTC). These orders remain active for 30, 60, or 90 days from entry, or until you cancel it.

Ordered does not mean executed. Your online order can fall victim to delays in execution. Market orders will generally be filled quickly, but high trading volume, market volatility, and system glitches can delay even these orders.

PLAY MONEY

You can experience all the aspects of online trading with simulators such as *The Game* from E-Trade. This program opens an online account for you and funds it with $100,000 of play money. You use the play money to buy and sell stock under real-time conditions. This way, you can experiment with online investing, and learn from your mistakes without risking real money. Find *The Game* at www. etrade.com.

Verify Stock Order

ELOQUENT INC			NASDAQ(NM): ELOQ		as of Sep 29, 2000 12:34:03 PM ET	
Last	Change	% Change	Volume		Bid	Ask
$2^7/_8$	$-^1/_8$	-4.17	69,500		$2^3/_4$	$2^{15}/_{16}$
Open	Prev. Close	Low	High		Bid Size	Ask Size
$2^{15}/_{16}$	3	$2^3/_4$	3		200	1,100
Last Size	Tick Trend	P/E Ratio	Quote Condition		Option Symbols	
3,500	-==+-+=	-6.25	Downtick - Restricted			

---

stock | option | buy fund | redeem fund

STOCK ORDER   **PREVIEW**

Account	Account Type
Demo Account (63010425)	Margin

Transaction	Quantity	Symbol & Co. Name	Price	Term
Buy	400	A	Market	DAY
		AGILENT TECHNOLOGIES INC		
	Time	Est. Commission	Est. Total Order	
	05:18:46PM (ET)	Free	$19,575.00	

IMPORTANT:
Please review order carefully.

NOTE: Click only once to place your order
[PLACE ORDER] [CANCEL ORDER]

Quotes are not delayed.					
Last Price:	48.9375	Bid:	0.0156	Ask:	96.6250
Change:	+0.9922	Day's High:	49.7500	Day's Low:	47.8125

TRACKING YOUR PORTFOLIO PERFORMANCE

Portfolio tracking screens allow you to see the overall value of your investment portfolio and the value of your individual holdings. Your holdings are listed and you can view your performance at any time.

FIND TRACKING TOOLS

With online investing, you no longer need to check stock prices through the newspaper. Even the most basic online brokerage accounts give you a portfolio tracking screen. This screen allows you to view a full list of your account holdings and information about each item, such as its current price, its total value, and what profit or loss you're showing since the time you bought it.

Some broker's portfolio trackers may include a *watch list*. This is a system of pop-up bulletins with news flashes or important price points of stocks you don't own but want to watch.

Update frequency. Brokers will update portfolio information for you, but the frequency of their updates varies from broker to broker. Some will update daily, some will update as trades are made, and some will offer updates throughout the day as stock prices change.

Free tracking elsewhere. If your broker offers only a basic portfolio service, you can still have the benefits of sophisticated tracking for free. Tracking services are offered at many financial websites, through Internet service providers, and through search engines. Visit www.quicken.com.

Bells and whistles. Some free portfolio trackers on the Internet come with advanced features that allow you to view and rank your stock holdings in multiple ways. For example, you can view your total overall gains and losses, view the day's gains or losses and price movement, get real-time updates, view your holdings' present price-to-earnings (P/E) ratios and asset values, or customize the pages to contain nearly any kind of information you want. Quicken.com even shows the diversity of your portfolio.

> **26** You can find investment recordkeeping requirements online with the IRS at www.irs.gov. Click on "Publication 550."

WATCH THE NEWS

To get the most from your portfolio screens, pay attention to news about your individual holdings and learn about the internal workings of the company. Your portfolio tracker should include a news link that will alert you to breaking news about the companies you own. If the portfolio screen provided by your broker doesn't have this feature, it's important to go to another site and set up a free tracker that does.

KEEP GOOD RECORDS

Keep an eye on your investments. This means not only with online screens but also with hard copy recordkeeping. Broker confirmations of each buy and sell trade, records of your money movements into and out of accounts, transfers, dividend records, and regular account statements will come to you through the regular mail. These are helpful in any dispute with the broker or the IRS. Some brokers let you choose to receive confirmations and statements online only, saving time and postage. You can protect yourself by printing out the information and keeping records on file.

▼ **HOW DO YOU MEASURE UP?**
With online investing, you can measure your performance whenever you wish, 24 hours a day, seven days a week.

Stocks & Related

Security	Security Description	Rating	Quantity	Price	Value
A	AGILENT TECHNOLOGIES INC	C-2-1-9	835	47.938	40,028
T	AT&T CORP COM	B-1-2-7	175	28.500	4,988
FISV	FISERV INC WISC PV 1CT	B-1-1-9	315	62.125	19,569
HWP	HEWLETT PACKARD CO DEL	B-2-1-7	1,900	103.813	197,244
INTC	INTEL CORP	B-2-1-7	400	44.438	17,775
RSTA	ROSETTA INPHARMATICS INC		400	28.000	11,200
WIND	WIND RIVER SYSTEMS INC		300	48.563	14,569

Total Stocks & Related   305,372

Mutual Funds

Security	Security Description	Rating	Quantity	Price	Value
CSTGX	AIM CONSTELLATION FUND CL A		217.5430	47.470	10,327
ALTFX	ALLIANCE TECHNOLOGY FUND CLASS A		103.4720	138.550	14,336
OTCBX	MFS MID-CAP GROWTH FD CL B		823.8820	18.310	15,085
MBNLX	ML MUNI BD NATIONAL PT B	N/A	4,161.7040	9.790	40,743

Total Mutual Funds   80,491

Total Portfolio Value   412,751

STOCK RESEARCH AND ANALYSIS

O nline investors have access to a cyberworld of investment-related information and analysis around the clock. You're the research and analysis department of your own online investing firm.

AT YOUR FINGERTIPS

Online researching is direct and effective. You no longer need to call your broker during business hours, make a request, then wait for faxed or mailed materials, that could be outdated, to arrive. The Internet gives you access to the types of financial information, technical analysis, news, and market indicators that were previously available only through a Wall Street firm.

AN OLD STANDBY

A reliable source of stock analysis is the Value Line Investment Survey. Most of the information on this company's website (www.valueline.com) is by subscription (freely accessed in print at your local library). There are also valuable free reports, stock and mutual fund analysis, and market news on the website.

FROM YOUR BROKER

Your online broker may carry many types of research and investment information on its website or even offer it to you as part of your account portfolio. This information generally consists of third-party research gathered from commercial research and news services or some variety of research conducted by the brokerage firm itself. In addition, many firms offer their own full-service research to accounts serviced at premium commission rates. Accounts with high balances are frequently offered premium research for free.

STRAIGHT FROM ▶ YOUR COMPUTER
Your computer can hand you a lot of analysis and research that used to be the sole domain of Wall Street firms.

FROM THE COMPANY ITSELF

You can research a company directly online. By going to a company's website you can view online, or request hardcopies of information such as the annual report, financial and equity statements, management profiles, balance sheets over the last few quarters, earnings, and projections about future business. You could also call the company's Investor Relations Department to ask questions if you prefer.

FROM YOUR ISP

Your Internet service provider (ISP) is likely to have a personal finance area on its home page or offer the option of having it on your personalized startup page. Links to research websites, basic investor education, and some surprisingly elaborate research and analysis can come to you just by staying home. Many ISPs also give you a personal portfolio page and a stock tracking system.

BACKUP SYSTEM

If you don't like taking the time to research investments and interpret information, you might consider backing up your low-commission online account with a full-service offline broker who will do the work and advise you. Then, you could use your low-commissioned online account for making some of your trades.

FROM THE GOVERNMENT

You may want to make your first stop the Securities and Exchange Commission (SEC). This organization regulates the securities industry and requires public companies to register with them. The SEC's EDGAR (Electronic Data Gathering Analysis and Retrieval) database at www.sec.gov/edgarhp.htm will tell you whether a company actually exists, and then offers you a lot of information about that company. You can view or download annual reports, insider trades, stock offering information, and various other types of reports.

Corporate document filings—everything from company bankruptcies to IPO filings—are easily accessed at 10K Wizard (www.tenkwizard.com). You can also read up-to-the-minute news about a company.

FUNDAMENTAL RESEARCH

M*ost investors take a fundamental approach to their investment strategies. They focus on the qualities that have traditionally indicated the future of a company, its industry, and the overall economy.*

WHAT IT IS

Fundamental analysis examines a company's financial strength and value. It also focuses on the economic climate surrounding the company itself and its operation. This analysis trys to determine what a company is worth today, and more importantly, what it might be worth in the future. Some of the factors it may look at are:

Earnings. Analysis of earnings includes the company's net income, its earnings per share, the price of the stock compared to the company's earnings (also called a P/E ratio), the current value of its shares, other appraisals of the company's value, and its prospects for growth;

Equity. Analysts look at the overall value of a company's shares within the markets. This gives them a measure of the company's strength relative to others. They also look to see whether company management has a significant investment in the company. This tells them how strongly management feels about the prospects for the company.

Revenues. Analysts will look at the company's income, expenses, assets, and cash flow. This shows how money is earned and used and indicates how well it's managed.

CONFERENCE CALLS

A new way for investors to stay in touch with a company's information is through a conference call over the Internet.

You can now listen in, for example, on a company's presentation to Wall Street of its latest earnings report—as it takes place. Wall Street professionals have been listening to these calls for years and use these reportings as first-hand financial information.

You can listen in live or through an archive of calls at websites such as CCBN's Street EventsOne investor website: www.ccbn.com. Click on "INDIVIDUAL INVESTOR CENTER."

Be aware that the information you receive in a conference call is subjective and may need to be interpreted and analyzed—just as most of the information on the Internet should be before you invest.

 27 A stock analysis screen at one website is not an end-all for research. Analyze details thoroughly.

MUTUAL FUND SCREENING PROGRAMS

You can use a screening program to find mutual funds that meet your parameters. Here are a few to try:

● Mutual Funds Online (www.mfmag.com);
● Forbes magazine's website www.forbes.com/tool/toolbox/lipper/screen.asp);
● Quote.com (www.quote.com/mutual_funds/index.html).

STOCK SCREENING PROGRAMS

Not crazy about analyzing fundamental information? A *stock screen* analyzes the criteria you put into it and returns choices based only on that specific criteria. A stock screen is basically a program that finds companies that match performance criteria you select. For example you might enter maximum and minimum parameters for a company's growth rate, price-earnings ratio, and revenue over a period of time. You might review a dozen or more criteria. Then the screening program sifts through its entire database of stocks and retrieves the ones that meet your standards. You can then ask the program to compare these companies based on how well each meets your criteria. Some brokerage sites may also have stock screens for clients. Some free sites are:

● www.stockscreener.com;
● www.marketplayer.com;
● Yahoo! finance at www.yahoo.com;
● www.quicken.com. This is a helpful site for evaluating a company's fundamentals;
● Multex Investor is a free supersite for research and analysis with access to over 300,000 investment reports and lots of analytical information (see http://multexinvestor.com).

Some of these websites require Adobe Acrobat reader.

TECHNICAL RESEARCH

Technical analysis focuses strictly on a stock's price movements using charts and graphs. Online investing gives you access to a wealth of technical research.

28 By printing out stock charts from the Internet, you can build a library of stock and market movements, and become familiar with technical patterns.

WHAT IT IS

Technical analysis is based on the belief that everything that happens in the real world will be absorbed by, and appear in the results of, a stock's price performance. That performance can then be viewed on a stock's *chart*, which is a graph of its prices over time. It's a system based on statistical analysis of stock price trends, with minimal emphasis on a company's actual business performance. Technical analysts may run computer models or work by pencil and pad, but all typically are looking to identify recurring patterns and developing ways to anticipate when those patterns will occur so they can take advantage of changes at the right times.

Technicians may focus on price highs and lows, price trends over certain time periods, the volume of shares traded in relation to price trends, or many other scenarios.

Statistical information involving price movements are usually most easily understood through a chart or graph which can dramatically illustrate patterns.

Some highly regarded analysts swear by certain systems; others call technical analysis voodoo. Investors should be cautious and thorough before following technical advice. Here are ways to monitor technical factors:

- Real-time quotes;
- Financial charts and graphs;
- Trends in stock prices;
- Buying and selling of a particular stock;
- Indexes showing the collective price movements of groups of stocks;
- Economic indicators designed to predict future price movements in the market as a whole.

THE FATHER OF TECHNICAL ANALYSIS

The theory behind technical analysis traces back to Charles Dow in the early 1900s. The Dow Jones Industrial Average was created out of Dow's theory of market analysis.

▲ MAKE YOUR OWN CHART

Many online brokers offer you the ability to customize technical charts based on your own criteria.

SOME SOPHISTICATED CHARTING

There are charts to show the effect of economic factors upon the price of stocks, indicators influencing the way groups of stock move, and charts based upon things like a company's relative strength—usually requires purchasing proprietary software or subscribing to a charting service. Prophet Finance (www.prophetfinance.com) has such online charting systems for a fee, but also provides extensive free charts, studies, trendlines, indexes, and indicators.

TAKE A TEST DRIVE

Technical charts and graphs view price movements in dozens of different ways. To explore the vast world of technical analysis and charting, visit websites such as:

- Equis (www.equis.com). Click on the "FREE" tab for a tutorial and access to charts;
- Big Charts (www.bigcharts.com);
- StockCharts (www.stockcharts.com);
- TradingCharts (www.tradingcharts.com);
- ClearStation (www.clearstation.com). It also has stock screens, news, and quotes.

The following two websites have technical stock screening programs that allow you to set parameters and find stocks that match your standards:

- Alpha Chart (www.alphachart.com/scan.html);
- Investorama (www.investorama.com/iqc_scan.html).

Another useful website, VectorVest, has stock screens that combine both technical and fundamental approaches to research (www.vectorvest.com).

OTHER RESEARCH

*E**ffective research is vital to investment success. There's so much financial information and tools on the Internet that it's important to know where and how to efficiently find them.***

WHERE TO LOOK

You may want to be attuned to both fundamental and technical factors. Together, they paint a total picture of a company you might consider as an investment.

You may also want to be in touch with what's happening in the overall market and the economy, and see how your investment choice compares with other companies in the same line of business or sector.

The answers are scattered all over the Internet in reports, analyses, charts, news, and interpretations. It's a broad spectrum, but there are many helpful sites that can take you into the specific areas.

You can find simple to elaborate financial websites giving you free online portfolios, access to fundamental and technical research, stock and broker ratings, and a wealth of links to further financial information. Smart Money (www.smartmoney.com), Money Magazine (www.money.com), and CNBC cable news network (www.cnbc.com) offer a wide variety of research and investment materials and a home page you can customize.

SEARCH ENGINES

Many Internet search engines can direct you to effective research websites and financial articles, but it's difficult—and annoying— to wade through all their ad hype in search of links to research information. For efficient financial researching, the best engines are often the ones with relatively few ads or blinking banners.

The Lycos Network (www.lycos.com/network) is a popular and well-organized *portal* that includes the Lycos search engine, HotBot engine, and Quote.com, a provider of excellent financial data, quotes and indexes for the U.S. and Canadian markets.

Dogpile (www.dogpile.com) is a clean and easy-to-use metasearch engine with their own directory, along with scans of major and many less-known search engines supplying links.

Street Index (www.streetindex.com) is a compact, no nonsense directory of links to all types of stocks traded on the stock exchanges, along with insider news, IPOs, earnings, and index fund links.

MEGASITES AND SUPERSITES

Here are just some of the many sites available to you.

- **Wall Street Research Net**
  (www.wsnr.com). This website distributes a universe of extensive research and information to investors over the Internet. It gives you literally thousands of resources at your fingertips, and claims over 500,000 links to such information as SEC documents, company home pages, annual reports, market analysis, stock quotes, charting graphs, conference calls, global databases, and navigation to all major news websites and financial periodicals. It's a first stop and last resort to accessing anything to do with investment research.

- **InvestorGuide**
  (www.investorguide.com). Type in a stock symbol click "RESEARCH" to get research reports and charts, with well-organized links to a world of information. Unbiased and comprehensive, it also offers investor education, links to financial publication articles, news, and market analysis.

- **CNET**
  (www.cnet.com). This is a major financial website with news, charts, personal portfolio areas with tracking, quotes, and compilations of brokerages "buy" and "sell" ratings for stocks. You can link to almost anywhere from CNET to access reports and news, and then jump to other supersites.

- **Yahoo!**
  (www.quote.yahoo.com). This website is thought of as a general search engine, but Yahoo! Finance is better described as a huge financial website. There's enough quality research, reports, news, technical charts, analysis, links, and portfolio servicing to keep you anchored for hours. Yahoo! keeps adding services and has become a major financial presence on the Internet.

- **Investor Alley**
  (www.investorsalley.com). For researching overall market trends and seeing how various sectors (groups of companies in the same industry) are faring, this website runs the gamut from breaking news and editorials to research reports, analysis, and trend predictions.

- **The Financial Web**
  (www.financialweb.com). This supersite offers both fundamental and technical research along with services you might not be getting from a deep discount broker. It includes stock and options trackers, real-time quotes, charts, screens, company reports, and an online community.

- **Microsoft Money Central**
  (www.moneycentral.msn.com). This website has columns by insightful analysts as well as portfolio management reports. Check out the Stock Research Wizard and the mutual fund search tool.

ONLINE GRAPEVINE

O nline investors are bombarded by information and advice. Can you trust everything you see or hear?

NEWSLETTERS

There are thousands of financial newsletters online offering reports and recommendations. Most charge a subscription fee. A newsletter is the advice of one person, a research company, or at worst, one person masquerading as a company. Anyone can publish an investment newsletter—they are unregulated, so buyer beware. Short-term, free trials and word-of-mouth are the best ways to find quality, legitimate newsletters. Use the advice, however, as a starting point for your own research.

Check disclosures. Does the newsletter receive payments from companies for making investment recommendations? Look for specific disclosure statements at the end of articles, on a disclosure page, or on a FAQ page on the website. Payments to a newsletter publisher can take many forms. Take note of disclosures stating that the publisher "takes a position in the security from time to time" (has received or bought stock in the company) or has been "retained as an advisor" (is being paid a consulting fee) or other statements indicating the publisher has a connection or financial tie to or stake in the recommended company.

Check advice. Be wary of recommendations for buying into thinly-traded stocks and upstart companies. Research SEC filings and other sources before jumping on a hot new stock—unless you can take the risk of losing money.

Check complaints. The SEC's Enforcement Division (www.sec.gov/enforce.htm) lists watchdog actions taken against newsletters and financial advisors. The NASD (www.nasdr.com) also maintains a disciplinary list.

29 The first rule of bulletin boards is: Don't believe everything you read.

30 *Anyone* can start a newsletter or post analysis of a company on the Internet. Keep that in mind.

THE GRAPEVINE ▶
Remember that a grapevine acts a lot like the game of telephone. Stories get changed and embellished to serve the needs of the people relaying the information. Be critical about what you hear. Make sound decisions based on your own research, not on grapevine hearsay.

NEWSGROUPS

Investment newsgroups can provide useful starting points for research, but realize that most of these groups are expressing opinions and commentaries, not facts. Online newsgroups can turn into forums of exaggerated exchange. Also, beware of downloading materials from a newsgroup. It could contain a virus. DejaNews (www.dejanews.com) maintains extensive links to newsgroups online and lets you search the text of messages posted.

CHAT ROOMS

The good. Chat rooms give investors a chance to cybertalk about stocks, compare experiences in the market, air complaints about online brokers, and get solutions to common problems. Chats often feature top professionals who interact with investors online.

The bad. Chat rooms are comprised of individual's opinions. Don't take opinion for fact. Research any new information you get.

The ugly. Chats are easily disguised as helpful advice or off-the-cuff comments designed to manipulate you into a scam. Never react to chat advice, suggestions, or news without first researching it yourself.

BULLETIN AND MESSAGE BOARDS

Be skeptical of stock tips and news about a stock. Anyone can site a well-known analyst as a source, or quote a publication or study. Follow-up by researching the story or report yourself. Ask these questions:

- On the posting, is there a legitimate link to the analyst or publication quoted?
- Is the posted news accurate? Go to the originator and read the whole text yourself.

Possibly the most frequented financial message board on the Internet is the Silicon Investor board (www.techstocks.com). It focuses on technology stocks and e-business. Users read for free, but pay a fee to post. Be alert for subtle sales pitches disguised as news.

31 If someone touts a certain stock in a chat room, realize that person could be well paid to do so.

PROBLEMS AND PITFALLS

Online investing has allowed millions of investors new opportunities to take charge of their finances. With every opportunity come problems, responsibility, and risk.

TECHNOLOGY, TRADING, AND YOUR BROKER

Online investing accounts for nearly 50% of retail trading volume. The industry is still in its infancy, experiencing technological growing pains.

BREAKDOWNS AND DELAYS

Many aspects of computerized, Internet trading can experience problems and cause frustration. These include:

- Your own modem and computer;
- Internet access;
- Internet traffic;
- Your broker's trading system;
- Your broker's software.

A capacity problem or technical glitch in any of these areas could delay or even prevent you from making trades.

TOP TWO CONCERNS

As voiced by online investors:

- Speed of ordering and reliability;
- Downtime at a broker's site can range from a few minutes to a few days.

32 Know your trading options in advance in case you are unable to access your account.

POOR SERVICE

You may encounter issues such as:

- Busy signals at toll-free helplines;
- Slow or no e-mail answers to questions or complaints;
- No direct contact with a person or technician who can help.

Prevention. Do early comparison shopping. Before signing with an online broker, test the customer service system with phone calls and e-mail. Ask to speak directly to a customer service rep. Access the technical support area and pose a "what if" problem for them to solve.

TRANSFERRING YOUR ACCOUNT

If you want to switch brokers, be prepared to wait. If everything goes smoothly, the process will take two to three weeks.

Transfers could be delayed if you:

- Use the wrong transfer form;
- Transfer a margin account;
- Change from one type of investment account to another;
- Transfer a retirement account;
- Fail to supply copies of statements or documents asked for in the transfer form.

WATCH YOUR STEP ▶
Being aware of the potential pitfalls and problems can help you from getting tripped up unexpectedly.

IT'S A FACT

Website outages are common, but few industries are hurt as dramatically by them as online trading firms.

THE COMPLAINT CHAIN

Here are some things you can do:

- Talk to a customer service representative and ask for an explanation. Ask how the problem will be resolved. Keep notes;
- If you're dissatisfied with the initial reaction, call the customer service manager and state your complaint;
- If you're still dissatisfied, write to the firm's corporate headquarters. Explain the problem, how you want it resolved, whether any promises were made to you, and ask for a reply in writing;
- Still dissatisfied? Contact the SEC, NASD, or your state Attorney General's office. Mail your complaint with copies of your letters to the broker.

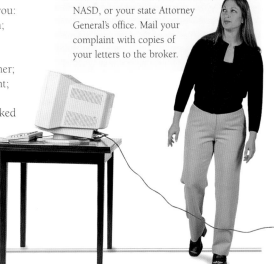

MISTAKES: THE OOPS! FACTOR

I n the eyes of many new investors, online investing is fun. However, you will run into problems if you don't take it seriously.

TOO MUCH TRADING

The ease and novelty of online investing can lead even experienced investors into a trap—using online investment accounts as entertainment. It's easy to be swept into trading in a way that doesn't match your specific goals and risk tolerances.

A Securities Industry Association (SIA) survey found that online investors tend to make more than twice the number of trades per year that strictly offline investors make. A University of California, Davis, study found that the increased trading actually resulted in lower earnings for active online investors when compared to investors who trade with a buy-and-hold style. One reason may be that trading for fun can lead to dabbling in speculative investments which may lead to less profit.

Prevention. Be a disciplined investor. There are less expensive forms of entertainment than online investing.

HUMAN ERROR

Be conscious of what you're doing on your online ordering screen, and stop to look at the "Order Preview" that appears after you enter an order. This is your only chance to correct or cancel a mistake that could cost you a lot of money. A trade that's been executed can't be cancelled. The mistake, therefore, is yours alone.

Prevention. Take nothing for granted. Any mistake in the little "no-brainer" tasks you perform on the computer will cost you. Be "brains-on" as well as hands-on.

NOT KNOWING THE TERRITORY

Do you know the difference between a limit order and a stop order? A company's revenue and it's equity? A common error is to jump into the market without truly knowing the concepts and terminology of investing that will help you navigate successfully.

Prevention. Basic education in the principles of investing can help avoid mistakes in an unforgiving environment.

33 If you place a market order on a volatile stock in a fast-moving market, you may be surprised at the price you receive.

RUNAWAY PRICING

Your market order will be filled at the price the stock is trading when the order is executed. When you place an order to buy or sell, don't assume that the trade occurs instantly. If you place a market order overnight, prices may be dramatically different by the time trading resumes the next morning.
Prevention. Use limit orders and stop orders when price is important. While limits and stops may not always be filled, that possible consequence will protect you from unhappy surprises.

DUPLICATE ORDERS

You clicked ORDER but the transaction didn't go through...or did it? Some broker's order confirmation screens can leave you wondering whether your trade was actually completed. Don't reenter your order.
Prevention. A click on the ORDER HISTORY or OPEN ORDER button should give you status updates on your order. Investors who overlook this feature might mistakenly assume their order wasn't filled and reenter it. In that case, they would end up duplicating the order and be responsible for two trades. Watch it on sales, too, or you could sell short.

CANCELLED ORDERS

An order is cancelled only when the market receives a valid cancellation order, not when you press CANCEL on a confirmation screen or portfolio screen.

A broker's system may flash a "Cancel Confirmed" notice to you. This only means that your request to cancel was received—not that the trade was actually stopped. Don't, therefore, go back and reenter a trade under the automatic assumption that your cancel order was actually cancelled. Follow up first.
Prevention. Ask your broker how you can ensure or confirm that a cancellation order actually worked.

THE THRILL IS GONE

If you lose interest in investing, your investments are less likely to grow. Long after the thrill of a new endeavor fades away, you still have a portfolio—and a future—to manage. Manage your portfolio consistently, and be aware of how your assets are allocated. A diverse, updated portfolio is key to successful investing.
Prevention: Know yourself and have a goal. Seeing a purpose for your activities will keep you enthused over the long-term.

SCAMS AND FRAUDS

The Internet offers great investment opportunities. It also gives scams and frauds a new operating arena.

OLD SCAMS IN A NEW MEDIUM

As people have become more savvy about investing, investment fraud and scams have become more sophisticated. You may be lured by flashy websites, electronic postings, and lies sent by e-mail.

Pump and dump. These scams take on new life in Internet chat rooms and as threads on bulletin boards. An "investor" hypes (pumps) a stock or "company employees" post threads about a stock in order to encourage buying and boost the price. The scammer then sells (dumps) the stock at an inflated price. The reverse ploy is to talk down a stock and profit from short-selling.

Pyramid schemes. These often take the form of e-mail, with come-ons such as "Make Big Money From Your Home Computer."

Affinity group frauds. These claim that because you're a member of a specific religion, ethnic group, or profession, you can take part in a special investment, trust, or annuity available only to that group. Investments in precious metals and foreign currencies are commonly used in this type of scam.

BEING AWARE

The Fraud Bureau (www.fraudbureau.com) is an informative free service established to alert and educate investors about fraud. The NASAA website (www.nasaa.org) has lists of state securities regulators. These state officials police the security industry in your state. The SEC actively pursues fraud and welcomes investor inquiries (www.sec.gov).

"WE'RE NOT REQUIRED TO REGISTER WITH THE SEC"

The following companies must file reports with the SEC:

- All U.S. companies with more than 500 investors and $10 million in net assets;
- All companies that list their securities on Nasdaq or a major exchange such as the NYSE. Investing in thinly-traded companies that are not widely known, and companies that don't file regular reports with the SEC may invite serious financial losses.

WAYS TO AVOID SCAMS

Before responding to any online investment opportunity, look for signs of a possible scam, such as:

- Claims that the investment is IRA Approved. No government agency approves investments for IRAs;
- Matchmaking offers that promise to match investment opportunities with your personal interests;
- Offers of offshore or tax-free investments;
- Requests for personal and financial information to determine if you qualify for the investment;
- Requests for a fee or deposit before full information about the investment can be released;
- Sponsors of a financial research website who may give biased—or false—information. Research and news are only as good as the facts supporting them.

DON'T TRUST BLINDLY

Be wary of promises of quick profits and inside information. If someone is excited about a certain stock in a chat room, realize that the person could be well-paid to do so. Be careful with promoters who use aliases. Find out who is running the operation. Question confidential information and insider quotes posted on a bulletin board or by a newsgroup. Request that any information and a prospectus be mailed to you. Never buy in to these types of offers directly online.

HOT SPOTS FOR INTERNET INVESTMENT FRAUD

- Spam e-mail
- Online newsletters
- Message boards
- Online newsgroups
- Chat rooms
- Fraudulent websites

GET THE FACTS

Ask and get answers to these questions before investing:

- **Is the investment registered?** Some types of small companies aren't required to register with the SEC. Your state securities regulator and the NASAA will have information about any legitimate company issuing stock;
- **Is the seller of the investment licensed?** Firms and individuals selling investments should be licensed for business in your state. The NASD has this information, as does your state securities regulatory agency. Check with the Better Business Bureau in the state where the investment seller is registered;
- **Does the investment sound too good to be true?** Don't believe in guaranteed or risk-free returns, or claims of astronomical returns over a short period of time;
- **Should you accept the offer on faith?** Never. Protect your money.

ADVANCED TOPICS

There's a big difference between online investing, online trading, and day trading. This chapter introduces you to the basics of day trading. It won't make you an expert.

DAY TRADING

Day trading turns the capital markets into a casino. It's not for inexperienced investors. The day trader locates stocks that are changing in price rapidly, buys them in large blocks, then sells out as soon as the price goes up a fraction of a point.

WHAT IT IS

Day traders follow the price movements of one or several stocks, hoping that their prices will rise and fall quickly so they can turn a quick profit. A committed day trader may make a hundred trades in a day, or maybe only one or two. It all depends on the trader's strategy.

WHAT ARE DAY TRADING FIRMS?

Day trading firms specialize in day trading. They're services offering direct access trading. They don't charge you for equipment and software, but require hefty startup balances in your account. They usually require $50,000-$75,000 as a basic acceptable starting point. You will also pay a small per share fee on trades, or a portion of the profits on your trades.

Some firms urge you to take training sessions costing thousands of dollars. They warn that you will most likely lose your initial investment before you make any money. They may also offer remote access accounts enabling you to trade from your home computer.

HOW IT WORKS

You can day trade from your broker's online account order screen but it's not very efficient. In day trading, it's best to directly access the bid/ask lists on ECNs and Level ll screens (see pgs. 68-69) through a broker who focuses on frequent traders. Specialized software systems allow you to *hit* (accept) a specific trader's price. It's a quick game. The key is to get in or out at a profit before anyone else can. Trading is usually done on margin—borrowed money—adding to the risk.

Day trading uses special tools such as technical analysis charts (and the skills to interpret them), discipline, intensity, focus, and quick reflexes. It's not as simple as sitting at a computer, watching price changes, and buying and selling at the click of a mouse. You may have to be switching through multiple order books, manipulating advanced software, and trying to separate fact from fiction from the information posted on your screens.

▲ TAKING A GAMBLE

Day trading is a tough game for small investors to win. But if you want, you can get a feel for day trading in free online day trading competitions at The Investor's Network Cafe (www.investnetcafe.com) and through The Rookie DayTrader (www.rookiedaytrader.com).

GOING DIRECT TO THE MARKET

As online trading becomes more mainstream, investors and day traders are insisting on getting the best possible price with every transaction. Some brokers pool orders and send them through *market makers*, who often shave a fraction of a point off the price and make a profit on your trade. Brokers who appeal to frequent traders bypass the market makers, allowing customers direct access to *electronic communications networks* (ECNs)—the order books where the trades are made. You can view the order book for a particular Nasdaq stock at www.island.com, the online home of one of the larger ECNs.

TOOLS OF THE TRADE

You need specific tools to be able to day trade. Your equipment needs to be more sophisticated and your software specific to the type of trading you want to do. Here's what you would need to have.

HARDWARE

You can day trade from your computer at home, but it will take increased bandwidth, special trading software, a trading account with a broker who caters to day traders, and sometimes a direct connection to that broker. A second (and sometimes third) monitor will help you keep an eye on the quote books for the stocks that you're following.

It's tough to be a day trader without a fast connection, whether that's DSL or cable, even T1 or T3. Most online brokers who focus on frequent traders offer their customers direct access to ECNs, and access to Level II quotes. These, however, don't currently match the sophistication of the full systems. If you think of the online broker's system as a keyboard, then the full system is a space flight control panel.

SOFTWARE

You also need to develop a trading system, which helps you recognize the statistical movements in a stock's price.

- Equis (www.equis.com) publishes MetaStock Professional, a technical analysis program that identifies statistical trends in a stock's price;
- Omega Research offers Tradestation, and the online version Tradestation.com, for developing and testing trading strategies.

Using one of these programs will cost you a hefty up-front fee, plus monthly charges for up-to-the-minute prices.

34 Day traders need a fast computer and a dedicated connection to the Internet.

Basic Techniques

Day trading techniques are the topic of week-long seminars and dozens of books, websites and newsletters. There are just a couple of basics, though and the rest of the techniques are refinements.

● Pick a small number of stocks–no more than five–that you will follow closely. These stocks should consistently be in the top 20-50 in terms of volume (number of shares traded per day), and have an intraday price range of 2 or more points;

● Study these stocks religiously, understanding what makes them move. Learn who the market makers are and watch their patterns;

● Develop a trading system and test it against historical data;

● Start with small lots (100-200 shares at a time) to gain confidence in your system before stepping up to large lots.

Caution!

● Day trading is not investing;
● Day trading can be highly stressful and very expensive;
● The vast majority of day traders lose money.

Market Conditions

Day trading is best accomplished in a market that has plenty of price movements. A flat market, where prices aren't going up or down very much, doesn't typically provide many opportunities to get in and get out quickly with a profit. If the overall market seems to be flat, there still may be plenty of opportunities within more narrow areas of the market, such as a particular sector (for example, high tech or financial services) or a particular group (such as small cap stocks, which are stocks of relatively small companies).

35
The day trader is thrust into a cyber-environment of multiple screens, flashing colors, and fast-changing numbers. Be sure that's for you.

SEEING THE MARKET FIRST-HAND

You can monitor every market move as it happens, analyze it, and make instant decisions—if you're sharp and quick.

THE POWER OF TRANSPARENCY

Until recently you couldn't see how many buyers were looking to buy shares of a particular stock at any given time. You couldn't see how many sellers were willing to sell either. You also couldn't see how many shares were available for trading or at what prices. There was no way for you to watch the constant push-pull, tug-o'-war between buyers and sellers and try to anticipate the next moves of the market. You could only watch a delayed stock ticker or ask your broker.

Today, with screens such as Level II screens and electronic order books, the so-called *order flow* in any stock is transparent to everyone, so you can follow every order placed for a stock.

Most of all, with these screens, you can decide which buyer or seller to trade with, whether it's a stock specialist on a major exchange, a market maker on Nasdaq, or another trader on one of the ECNs. Your broker must still do the physical placing of the order, but you can do virtually all the rest.

INTC

LAST   42 1/16
TIME   14:03:31
VOL   2,514,695

Shares	Buy Price	Shares	Sell Price
1,000	42 1/16	900	42 1/8
400	42 1/16	18	42 1/4
100	42 1/32	1,000	42 1/4
1,000	42 1/64	700	42 1/4
1,000	42 1/64	300	42 1/4
1,000	42 1/64	400	42.36
100	42 1/64	120	42 3/8
100	42 1/64	360	42 15/32
100	42 1/64	500	42.49
1,000	42 1/256	100	42.49
500	42	504	42 1/2
600	42	19	42 1/2
200	42	40	42 1/2
1,000	42	60	42 1/2
100	42	500	42 1/2
(994 more)		(1,637 more)	

As of 14:03:34

▲ ELECTRONIC ORDER BOOK
This screen from the ECN, Island, shows the system's order flow: the current bid and ask quotes, the number of shares involved in the offer to buy or sell, and the price at which the trader is willing to make a deal.

Full real-time quotes
These are displayed including the price of the last filled order, high and low prices of the day and the past year, trading volume and the last up/down tick.

Past executions
Past executions of the stock are shown by price, lot size, and where the order was executed.

Level II quotes
The Level ll quotes of buy and sell offers waiting to be filled. Similar prices will normally be grouped and color-coded. The name of the market maker or ECN offering the price is also listed.

Custom watch list
A Custom stock watch list that allows you to track a number of stocks' price movements at a glance.

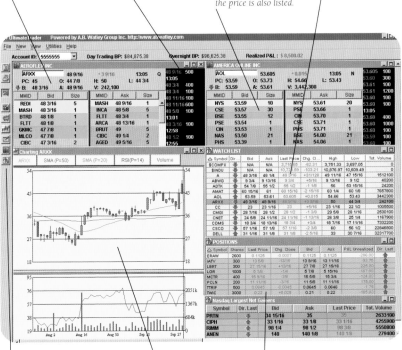

Order screen
Your ordering screen is incorporated as a panel which will allow you to send your order to the market or ECN of your choice. You directly type in the order and select where you want it to go. In a true day trade, the brokerage does not direct where the orders are sent.

Technical charts
A variety of technical analysis charts are at your disposal.

Current positions
A position reminder showing your current holdings and the immediate gains and losses you have on the trading you've been doing.

AFTER-HOURS TRADING

*A**lthough it sounds so basic, there's more to after-hours than trading.***

WHAT IT ISN'T

After-hours trading doesn't mean placing your buy or sell order onto your online broker's account screen at 11:00 p.m. for it to be filled the next morning when the market opens.

WHAT IT IS

After-hours trading trading is an uncertain cybermarket that's open for a few hours before and after the normal market times (9:30 a.m. - 4:00 p.m. Eastern time). After-hours trading combines a little of online investing with a lot of the price-grabbing gamesmanship of day trading. You can access the market through your online broker, make a trade at a decent price and exit, or you can stick around and get wrapped up in a day trading game of bidding, bluffing, buying, and going boom or bust.

HOW IT WORKS

You trade through your online account. If your online broker allows after-hours trading, you will use its after-hours ordering system giving you access to the ECN to which it subscribes.

You may be at a technological disadvantage because many professional traders will be using sophisticated software and advanced trading platforms that are unavailable to you at home.

After-hours trading has become a high-risk "game" played on ECN order books where "players" enter the prices at which they're willing to trade. Below is a very simplified example. The real thing is much more complicated and difficult.

AN EXAMPLE

1. You have a goal in mind to buy or sell a certain stock at a specific price, hoping to profit on the stock's price later.

2. You input your stock price onto the ECN order book and wait for someone to accept it.

3. Someone inputs a counter-price close to what you want. Do you take the counter-price (which means inputting another offer at that price, while your first offer is still live) or hold on?

THE WILD WEST

If online investing is a new frontier for you, after-hours trading will be like entering the wild west. After-hours trading presents added risks:

- The spreads between the buy and sell offers will likely be larger than you're used to seeing;

- You will be competing for prices against seasoned day traders with faster execution technology, a more complete picture of the market, and street-smart knowledge;

- Some stock prices may move greatly while others don't move at all;

- Rumors and late-breaking news about a stock can trigger larger-than-normal price shifts;

- The actions of one or a few traders can have a disproportionately large affect on a stock's price;

- NYSE listed stocks may not be available to trade;

- Frequently, more than one billion shares are traded on Nasdaq during normal market hours each day. A busy ECN may average only five million shares during an after-hours trading period. This low volume (called a *thinly traded market*) can make for exaggerated stock moves and creates a ripe environment for "pump and dump" manipulation of prices (where someone—or group—try to drive up a stock's price then sell their shares before everyone else does).

After-hours trading has been around only since late 1999. As it matures, the trading should become more stable, providing a less risky environment for the small investor. In the meantime, tread carefully.

4. Meanwhile, other prices are popping up on the ECN.

5. Anything you do will trigger other traders to do something too. You may end up with no one wanting to trade at your price and your order(s) go unfilled. You could also be maneuvered into buying more than you wanted at prices you didn't want.

IT'S A FACT

One reason for extending market hours was so investors could buy and sell stocks at times more convenient for them than the normal 9:30 a.m. to 4:00 p.m. (or 6:30 a.m. to 1:00 p.m. Pacific time) market hours.

INDEX